BOXERS

by Tammy Gagne

Consultants: Dianne Kurschner
and Jodie Alwin
Officers,
Northwoods Boxer Club

Capstone press®

Mankato, Minnesota

Edge Books are published by Capstone Press,
151 Good Counsel Drive, P.O. Box 669, Mankato, Minnesota 56002.
www.capstonepub.com

Library of Congress Cataloging-in-Publication Data
Gagne, Tammy.
    Boxers / by Tammy Gagne.
    p. cm. — (Edge books. All about dogs)
    Includes bibliographical references and index.
    Summary: "Describes the history, physical features, temperament, and
care of the boxer breed" — Provided by publisher.
    ISBN 978-1-4296-3365-9 (library binding)
    1. Boxer (Dog breed) I. Title. II. Series.
SF429.B75G34 2010
636.73 — dc22   2008054785

Editorial Credits
Jennifer Besel and Molly Kolpin, editors; Veronica Bianchini, designer;
    Marcie Spence, media researcher

Photo Credits
Alamy/Celia Mannings, 16; Mary Evans Picture Library, 9
Capstone Press/Karon Dubke, cover, 1, 10 (bottom), 13, 18, 19, 22, 23,
    25, 26, 27, 29
Corbis/Historical Picture Archive, 10 (top)
Friederun von Miram-Stockmann, 12
Shutterstock/cynoclub, 21; david woodberry Pure Eye Photo, 24;
    George Lee, 5, 6; Julie Richards, 15
UK Boxer Dogs, 11

Printed in the United States of America in Stevens Point, Wisconsin.
122010   006019R

Table of Contents

Bouncing Boxers 4

Boxer History 8

A Sturdy Breed 14

Caring for a Boxer 20

Glossary 30

Read More 31

Internet Sites 31

Index 32

CHAPTER 1

BOUNCING BOXERS

With its square jaw and wrinkled face, the boxer looks like a very serious dog. But don't let the boxer's look fool you. The truth is that boxers are one of the most fun-loving dog breeds. Owners often use words like "clownish" and "playful" to describe their dogs.

Young boxers are especially known for having loads of energy. They love to bounce around and run. Once a boxer is about 3 years old, it usually calms down a bit. But most boxers remain playful as adults. Boxers are even named for their playfulness. The breed received its name because the dogs move their feet like boxers in a ring while playing.

Playing fetch is a great way for a boxer to work off its playful energy.

EDGE FACT

In 2008, a boxer named Presley earned the title of Greatest American Dog on a TV show of the same name.

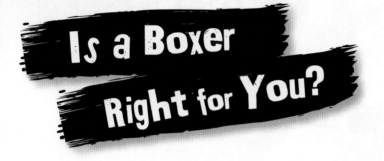

Is a Boxer Right for You?

Boxers can adapt to almost any surrounding. They can live in cities, suburbs, or rural areas. What matters most to a boxer is that there are people nearby. Boxers rely heavily on human companionship.

Regular exercise is very important to the high-energy boxer. Many owners walk or run their boxer just before leaving home for long periods of time. This helps tire the dog so it naps while the owners are gone.

If this breed is right for you, the best place to buy a boxer puppy is from a breeder. Breeders take care to ensure the dogs are healthy. You also can adopt an adult boxer through a rescue group or animal shelter. Many healthy, loving boxers are abandoned each year. Rescue groups help these dogs find new homes.

CHAPTER 2

BOXER HISTORY

The boxers we know today were developed in Germany. Historians believe boxers are related to several other dog breeds. These include the bulldog, the bullmastiff, and the Staffordshire bull terrier. Like these other breeds, boxers were used for hunting in Europe in the 1600s. A boxer's strong jaws could hold down a powerful boar or even a small bear.

In the late 1700s, people used boxers in bullbaiting events throughout Europe. In bullbaiting contests, boxers were trained to attack a bull. The dog would bite down on the bull's nose and hold on for as long as it could. But many people thought bullbaiting was cruel. They fought to make it illegal. It was outlawed in the early 1800s.

Early boxers were trained to fight in bullbaiting competitions.

Owners used early boxers to help them hunt badgers and other animals.

By the late 1800s, people were beginning to appreciate the boxer as much for its proud look as for its hunting skills. Breeders formed the German Boxer Club in Munich, Germany, in 1895. The club held its first dog show in 1904. At this time, boxers were bred to be taller, more athletic, and more elegant looking than earlier dogs in the breed.

The first boxer **breed standard** was created by the founders of the German Boxer Club. The boxer standard that most kennel clubs use today is very similar to the original document.

Boxers in the early 1900s were bred for their elegant look.

breed standard — the physical features of a breed that judges look for in a dog show

Hunting and competing in dog shows weren't the only jobs early boxers held. German soldiers used boxers during times of war. Boxers carried messages from one group of soldiers to another. Some boxers transported communication wires during World War I (1914–1918) and World War II (1939–1945). These boxers wore spools of wire that unwound as the dogs moved across the land. Boxers were also one of the first breeds used as police dogs in Germany.

Modern-day boxers are rarely used for hunting. Today's working boxers serve as police dogs or guide dogs. Many modern boxers are also kept simply as pets.

German soldiers trained boxers during World War I.

Making a Name for Themselves

Boxer enthusiasts imported the first boxers to the United States in the early 1900s. But most Americans did not take notice of the breed.

In the 1940s, boxers began to make a name for themselves. Many boxers won Best in Show titles at Westminster, a famous dog show in New York.

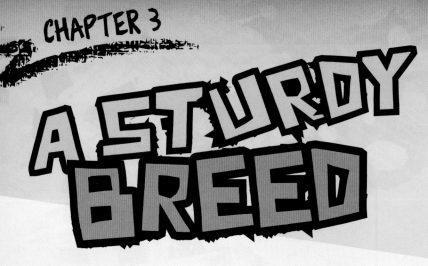

CHAPTER 3

A STURDY BREED

Some dog breeds are elegant. Others are intelligent. Boxers have both of these qualities.

Boxers are medium-sized dogs. Most males stand 23 to 25 inches (58 to 64 centimeters) tall at the **withers**. Females are slightly shorter. They usually stand between 21 ½ to 23 ½ inches (55 to 60 centimeters) tall. A show dog may be a little bigger or smaller. An overall look of good **proportion** is what matters most.

A Wrinkly Face

A boxer's head looks like a wrinkly box. You can see the wrinkles on the forehead best when the dog's ears are standing upright. The wrinkles on each side of the muzzle are always visible. Many people think the side wrinkles give the boxer its thoughtful expression.

The breed's dark brown eyes also play an important part in its appeal. A boxer's eyes are said to mirror the feelings of anyone who looks into them.

Boxers often look like they are deep in thought.

withers — the top of an animal's shoulders

proportion — when one body part is not larger than another

Boxers come in two color combinations. They may be fawn or brindle. Fawn dogs range from light tan to red-brown. A brindle coat is made up of either black stripes on a fawn background or fawn stripes on a dark brown background. Both fawn and brindle boxers may also have white markings. According to the American Kennel Club (AKC), a show dog's white markings should cover no more than one-third of its body.

A boxer's coat is short, smooth, and shiny. You can see the dog's muscles easily through this kind of coat. But though they have short hair, boxers still shed. They shed the most hair in the spring and fall.

fawn

brindle

Boxers have short, shiny coats.

Docking and Cropping

Most breeders dock their boxers' tails. Tail docking involves cutting away the end of a dog's tail soon after the puppy is born. In some countries tail docking has been outlawed.

Many breeders in the United States also crop, or cut away, the outer parts of the ear in the dog's first weeks of life. Cropping makes the dog's ears stand upright. An **anesthetic** is used, so the process isn't painful for the puppy. For some dog breeds, ears must be cropped if a dog is entered in AKC dog shows. Boxers, however, may have uncropped ears and still compete in shows with no penalty.

Ear cropping and tail docking were originally done to keep the ears and tail from being injured when a dog was hunting. Today the operations are done to keep the traditional look.

EDGE FACT

Almost one-third of boxers with a lot of white in their coats are deaf.

anesthetic — a drug that makes animals sleep
so doctors can perform surgery on them

Temperament

You couldn't ask for a more loyal pet than a boxer. Boxers bond with their human family members very closely. They especially love children. Boxers are very smart, but they can also be stubborn. Owners should begin training their boxers right away. If left untrained, boxers can be quite mischievous. It is much easier to teach a good behavior than correct an unpleasant one.

Boxers are extremely playful, and they have a natural love of jumping. Many will jump into the air to catch toys like flying discs. Boxers can be excited to the point of being overly friendly. Socializing your boxer is important. With good training, your dog will know how to behave around people and other dogs.

Boxers are loving and loyal pets.

CHAPTER 4

CARING FOR A BOXER

The boxer needs a moderate amount of care compared to other breeds. Boxers must get regular exercise. Their short coats need very little grooming. Owners must also provide their dogs with food and water every day. Simply spending time with this playful, loving breed is an important job too.

Training

As soon as you bring your boxer puppy home, enroll it in puppy kindergarten. Much like kindergarten for children, this beginner class will teach your dog basic manners. Dogs learn how to behave around people and other animals. They also learn basic commands like "come" and "sit."

Work with your boxer every day to help your dog remember the commands it has learned. Praise your pet whenever it does what you ask. Most boxers delight in pleasing their owners.

Boxers can make wonderful watchdogs. They are very protective of the people they love, especially children. But owners must train their dogs so they do not hurt anyone by mistake.

Boxers need to learn how to behave around people and other dogs.

EDGE FACT

Boxers usually live between eight and 10 years.

Feeding

Feed your dog a food made from quality ingredients. Lean meats and vegetables are as good for your dog as they are for you. Dogs need more fat in their diets than people do. But too much fat can be bad for your pet. Many types of high-quality dog foods can be found at pet supply stores.

Choosing the right food is important for the health of your dog.

Food labels usually include serving sizes, but some boxers need more or less food than the package suggests. Consider your dog's weight to make sure it is eating the right amount of food. As adults, male boxers should weigh between 65 and 80 pounds (29 and 36 kilograms). Females should weigh between 50 and 65 pounds (23 and 29 kilograms). If your boxer is extremely active, consider feeding it a food made for high-energy dogs. If your boxer is a couch potato, as some older ones are, it may need a diet formula.

Fun activity keeps your boxer healthy and happy.

EDGE FACT

Boxers enjoy chasing balls and other toys. However, not all boxers like returning these items to their owners.

Exercise

Give your boxer exercise by doing something you both enjoy. What you do is not nearly as important as making daily exercise a priority. A brisk walk is a healthy activity. But if you prefer running on the beach, take your dog with you. Be careful during hot days, though. Boxers overheat easily.

Regular exercise makes happy boxers. It also makes happy owners. Dogs with pent-up energy get into trouble. A boxer that doesn't get enough activity may exercise its teeth on your shoes or reduce your furniture to toothpicks!

Grooming

A boxer needs to be brushed at least once a week. Brushing removes dirt and dead hair from your dog's coat. Although a boxer's hair doesn't grow longer, it does shed. Owners will find a lot of dog hair in their homes if they don't regularly brush their boxers.

Unless your dog gets very dirty, it will need a bath only about once every two months. Dog shampoo can be purchased at a pet supply store. Never use your own shampoo on your boxer. It can dry out your dog's skin.

Trim your boxer's nails every two or three weeks. If you can hear your dog's nails when it walks, your pet is overdue for a clipping. You may be able to trim your dog's nails less often if it spends a lot of time outdoors. Walking on hard surfaces like pavement grinds an animal's nails naturally.

Your boxer's teeth should be brushed as often as possible. Perform this task every day if you can. Like its shampoo, your dog's toothpaste must be made only for dogs. Human toothpaste can make your pet sick.

Caring for Your Boxer

All boxers should see a veterinarian at least once a year. This annual checkup helps ensure that your dog is healthy. During a checkup, your vet will listen to your boxer's heart, examine its joints, and take its temperature. Your dog will also receive any necessary **vaccinations** at this time.

Talk to your vet about spaying or neutering your dog as soon as possible. These simple operations keep animals from producing offspring. Besides helping to control the pet population, the operations reduce boxers' risk for cancer and other illnesses.

Boxers tend to get cancer more often than many other dog breeds. Check your boxer regularly for any lumps or bumps on its body. Not all growths will be cancerous, but any tumor should be checked by a vet. If cancer is found early, many dogs can still live long lives.

Another common problem in boxers is an irregular heartbeat. If left untreated, it can lead to a heart attack and even death. Regular checkups can help catch an irregular heartbeat before it damages your dog's heart.

vaccination — a shot of medicine that protects animals from a disease

Care for your boxer properly, and affection will come back to you tenfold. Few breeds offer owners the boundless energy and love that a boxer does. If you can keep up with this lively breed, a boxer will fill your life with fun and friendship.

Vet checkups help catch health problems your dog might have.

Glossary

anesthetic (an-iss-THET-ik) — a drug that makes animals sleep so doctors can perform surgery on them

breeder (BREE-duhr) — someone who breeds and raises dogs or other animals

breed standard (BREED STAN-derd) — the physical features of a breed that judges look for in a dog show

muzzle (MUHZ-uhl) — an animal's nose, mouth, and jaws

neuter (NOO-tur) — a veterinary operation that prevents a male dog from producing offspring

proportion (pruh-POR-shuhn) — the relation of one part to another; boxers have good proportion when one body part is not larger than another.

socialize (SOH-shuh-lize) – to train to get along with people and other dogs

spay (SPEY) — a veterinary operation that prevents a female dog from producing offspring

vaccination (vak-suh-NAY-shun) — a shot of medicine that protects animals from a disease

withers (WITH-urs) — the top of an animal's shoulders; a dog's height is measured from the ground to the withers.

Read More

Green, Sara. *Boxers.* Dog Breeds. Minneapolis: Bellwether Media, 2009.

Landau, Elaine. *Boxers Are the Best!* The Best Dogs Ever. Minneapolis: Lerner, 2010.

Stone, Lynn M. *Boxers.* Eye to Eye with Dogs. Vero Beach, Fla.: Rourke, 2005.

Internet Sites

FactHound offers a safe, fun way to find Internet sites related to this book. All of the sites on FactHound have been researched by our staff.

Here's all you do:

Visit *www.facthound.com*

FactHound will fetch the best sites for you!

Index

adoption, 7
American Kennel Club
   (AKC), 13, 16, 17
appearance
   bodies, 4, 11, 14
   coats, 16, 17, 20, 26
   colors, 16, 17
   ears, 14, 17
   eyes, 14
   size, 14, 23
   tails, 17

breeders, 7, 11, 17
breed history
   and bullbaiting, 8, 9
   in Germany, 8, 11, 12
   and jobs, 8, 10, 11, 12
   in the United States, 13, 17

cropping, 17

docking, 17

exercising, 5, 6, 7, 20, 24, 25

feeding, 20, 22–23

grooming, 20, 26

life span, 21

personality. *See* temperament
puppies, 4, 7, 17, 20

socializing, 18, 21

temperament, 4, 5, 7, 14, 18,
   19, 20, 24, 29
training, 8, 9, 12, 18, 20

veterinary care, 28, 29